A DROP OF WATER

A BOOK OF SCIENCE AND WONDER

WRITTEN AND PHOTOGRAPHED BY

WALTER WICK

SCHOLASTIC INC.
New York Toronto London Auckland Sydney

ACKNOWLEDGMENTS

I would like to thank the following people for their invaluable help in the making of this book: Dan Helt and Kevin Williams, who assisted with the photography; Patricia Relf and Terese Kreuzer for help with the text; Paul A. Vetter, Ph.D., and Kathy Burkett for suggestions and for clarification of the science; Carol Devine Carson for the cover design; and my agent, Molly Friedrich, for her guidance.

I am also very grateful for the patience and expertise of my editors, Grace Maccarone and Bernette Ford, art director David Saylor, and all those at Scholastic who contributed to this project.

Finally, a special thanks to friends and family for their loving support.   —W.W.

Photograph on page 37, courtesy of NASA.

ISBN 0-590-02319-5

12 11 10 9 8 7 6 5 4 3 2 1   8 9/9 0 1 2 3/0

Printed in the U.S.A.   14

First Scholastic printing, October 1998

For Linda

We are going to spend an hour today in following a drop of water on its travels. If I dip my finger in this basin of water and lift it up again, I bring with it a small glistening drop out of the water below and hold it before you. Tell me, have you any idea where this drop has been? What changes it has undergone, and what work it has been doing during all the long ages water has lain on the face of the earth?

—ARABELLA B. BUCKLEY, 1878

WATER'S SMALLEST PARTS

A drop of water falls through the air. Down it splashes, breaking apart into tiny droplets. What would you see if you could break water into even smaller bits?

No matter how closely you look, you can't see water's tiniest parts. Like every other substance in the world, water is made of very tiny particles called molecules. On the pin above, the smallest droplet contains more than three hundred trillion water molecules.

PIN
ACTUAL SIZE

WATER'S ELASTIC SURFACE

Step by step, a camera reveals the curious changing shape of a drop of water as it falls from a spout.

The drop grows heavy and begins to fall. As it breaks from a strand of water, the drop shrinks itself into a round ball, or *sphere*. The drop flattens then elongates as it falls. The strand, meanwhile, breaks into tiny droplets. The impact of the drops hitting the water causes a new strand to bounce back out as another drop breaks away.

Because water molecules cling to each other like tiny magnets, a drop of water can stay in one piece, even as it falls through the air. But the molecules at the water's surface cling with a force that causes the surface to shrink. This force is called *surface tension*.

When the surface of a drop of water shrinks to its smallest size, the drop forms a sphere. The sphere stretches because of the drop's weight and motion, but surface tension helps keep the drop together, as if it were held in an elastic skin.

FLOATING STEEL
AND WILD WAVES

This steel pin seems to float magically on water. In fact, the pin is not really floating; it is held by the water's surface tension. This works only if the pin is very carefully lowered onto the water's surface. Otherwise the pin will sink.

An egg dropped from above transforms the calm surface of water into a wild wave. Immediately, surface tension forms wrinkles in the wave, breaks the jets of water, and shapes the smallest droplets into tiny spheres.

WHEN WATER MEETS AIR

A dry paintbrush is fluffy; the bristles of a wet paintbrush cling together. But the bristles of the paintbrush in this jar of water are wet *and* fluffy. Why do the two wet brushes behave in different ways?

The brush in the jar is held below the water's surface. Water surrounds the bristles, but has little effect on their positions. The wet brush outside the jar is surrounded by air. Water molecules don't cling to air, so they pull together and bring the bristles together, too. Of the two wet brushes, only the one outside the jar is affected by surface tension.

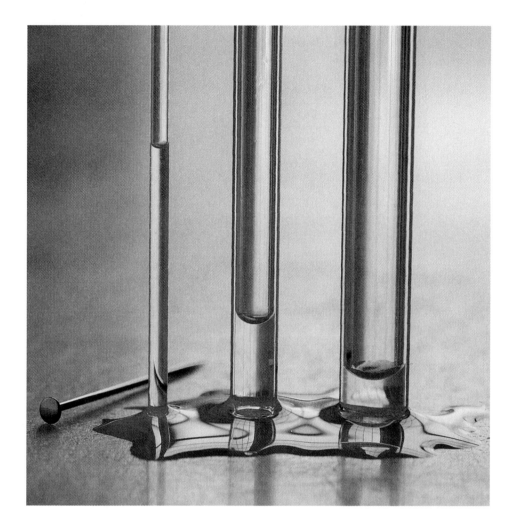

WHEN WATER FLOWS UP

Gravity causes water to flow downward, yet water has actually flowed up into these glass tubes. What could cause such strange behavior?

Water molecules cling to materials such as glass with an attractive force called *adhesion*. That's why water drops cling to windowpanes after a rain. This attraction is also what causes water to creep up the sides of the glass tubes. The narrower the tube, the higher water will climb. This behavior is called *capillary attraction*.

Anywhere water creeps through crevices—tiny spaces between grains of sand or fine veins in the stem of a plant—capillary attraction is at work.

SOAP BUBBLES

There are few objects you can make that have both the dazzling beauty and delicate precision of a soap bubble. Shown here at actual size, this bubble is a nearly perfect sphere. Its shimmering liquid skin is five hundred times thinner than a human hair.

Bubbles made of plain water break almost as quickly as they form. That's because surface tension is so strong the bubbles collapse. Adding soap to water weakens water's surface tension. This allows a film of soapy water to stretch and stretch without breaking.

When you blow a bubble, it looks somewhat like a drop of water emerging from a faucet. And just like the surface of a drop of water, the bubble's surface shrinks to form a sphere. Spheres and circles are mathematical shapes. Because they can form spontaneously, they are also shapes of nature. The circle below formed instantly when the film inside the loop of string was broken.

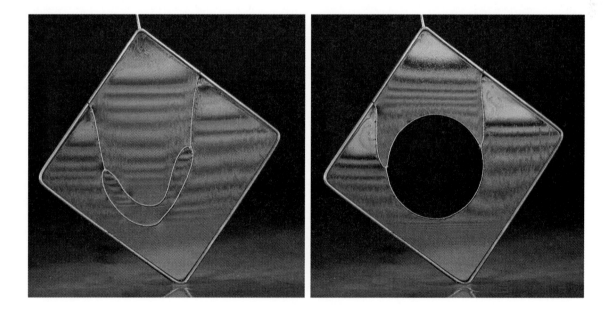

BUBBLE SHAPES

If you dip any wire frame into soap solution and pull it out, the wire edges will be connected with bubble film. The film shrinks, revealing the smallest possible surface area within the structure.

When this frame was pulled out of soap solution, twelve panels of bubble film connected at the center of the frame. A straw was used to blow a bubble in the center. The twelve panels pulled that inner bubble into the shape of a cube.

MOLECULES IN MOTION

If a drop of water is added to a jar of still water, and if the water in the jar is not stirred, where will the new drop go? Will it stay near the top or sink to the bottom? A simple experiment reveals the answer.

A drop of blue water enters a jar of clear water. It begins to split up. Parts of the drop sink and swirl in different directions. At last, the colored drop breaks into so many parts that it has become part of the whole jar of water.

The molecules in a liquid are moving all the time, pushing and pulling each other, attaching to and breaking away from neighboring molecules. The molecules in the blue drop break apart because they are pushed and pulled all over the jar by other water molecules. The energy that keeps the molecules moving is heat. This heat can come from the sun or the room in which the jar is standing. Without heat, water would not remain a liquid.

ICE

When water cools, it loses energy. The molecules slow down and eventually stop swirling and pushing each other. When water freezes, the molecules lock together, forming a rigid structure. A drop of blue water no longer moves. The water has changed from a liquid to a solid — ice.

Ice is a solid, like metal or rock. But, unlike metal or rock, ice is solid only at temperatures of 32 degrees Fahrenheit (0 degrees Celsius) or colder. At room temperature, ice melts, changing back to a liquid.

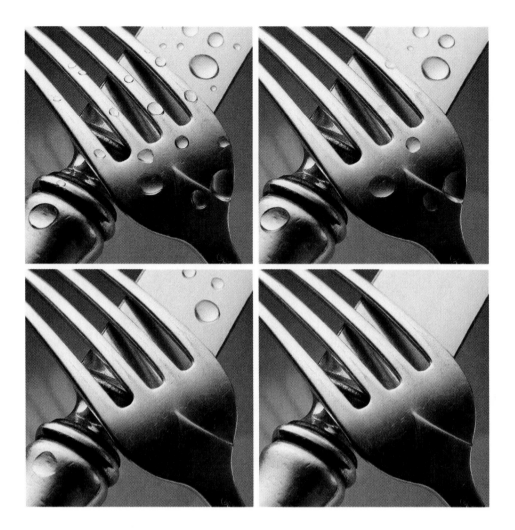

WATER VAPOR

Water always seems to be disappearing: from wet clothes on a line, from puddles on the ground, and from dishes on a draining board. We say it has dried up, but where has the water gone?

Just as water can be a liquid or solid, it can also be a gas. The water from the wet dishes *evaporates*. That is, it turns into a gas called *water vapor*. Molecule by molecule, the water from the drops on the wet dishes drifts invisibly into the air.

Heating water in a kettle speeds evaporation. Heat from the stove makes the water turn to steam, which is extremely hot water vapor. When the steam hits the cooler air, tiny droplets form, and we see a cloud just beyond the kettle's spout. Almost immediately, the droplets evaporate and change back to invisible vapor. Then the water molecules mingle with other molecules that make up air.

CONDENSATION

The air around us always contains some water vapor. Water molecules move rapidly through the air and hit everything in their paths. The molecules bounce off most warm surfaces, but stick to surfaces that are cold. In these photographs, molecules of water vapor stick to the coldest part of the glass. Gradually, droplets form on the glass as the molecules accumulate. Water vapor changes from a gas to a liquid; that is, it *condenses.*

EVAPORATION VERSUS CONDENSATION

In the photographs above, why do the water drops outside this glass disappear, while the drops inside remain?

Outside the glass, the water evaporates and spreads throughout the room as vapor. In time, the drops disappear. Inside the glass, water also evaporates, but the vapor is trapped. The air inside the glass becomes *humid*, which means that the air is full of water vapor. And that vapor condenses back onto the water drops as quickly as water molecules can evaporate. Therefore, the drops remain.

Remove the glass, and the vapor expands throughout the room. Evaporation continues, but condensation slows down. In time, the uncovered drops will disappear.

HOW CLOUDS FORM

Clouds are made of tiny water droplets, too small to be seen without a microscope. If a cloud droplet is to form, water vapor must first condense on a particle of dust. Carried by wind, these dust particles are often bits of pollen, soot, soil, or salt.

This experiment shows how cloud droplets form. Salt is placed on a jar lid above a dish of water. A glass cover traps the water vapor. In minutes, the vapor condenses on the salt and coats each grain with water. Hours later, the salt dissolves in the water drops.

Clouds form when water evaporates from the earth's surface and rises into colder air. There, the vapor condenses on cold, airborne particles. More and more molecules cling to the particles until droplets form. It takes about a million cloud droplets to make one raindrop. Rain does not taste salty or appear gritty because the particles that allow clouds to form are usually too small to be noticed in raindrops.

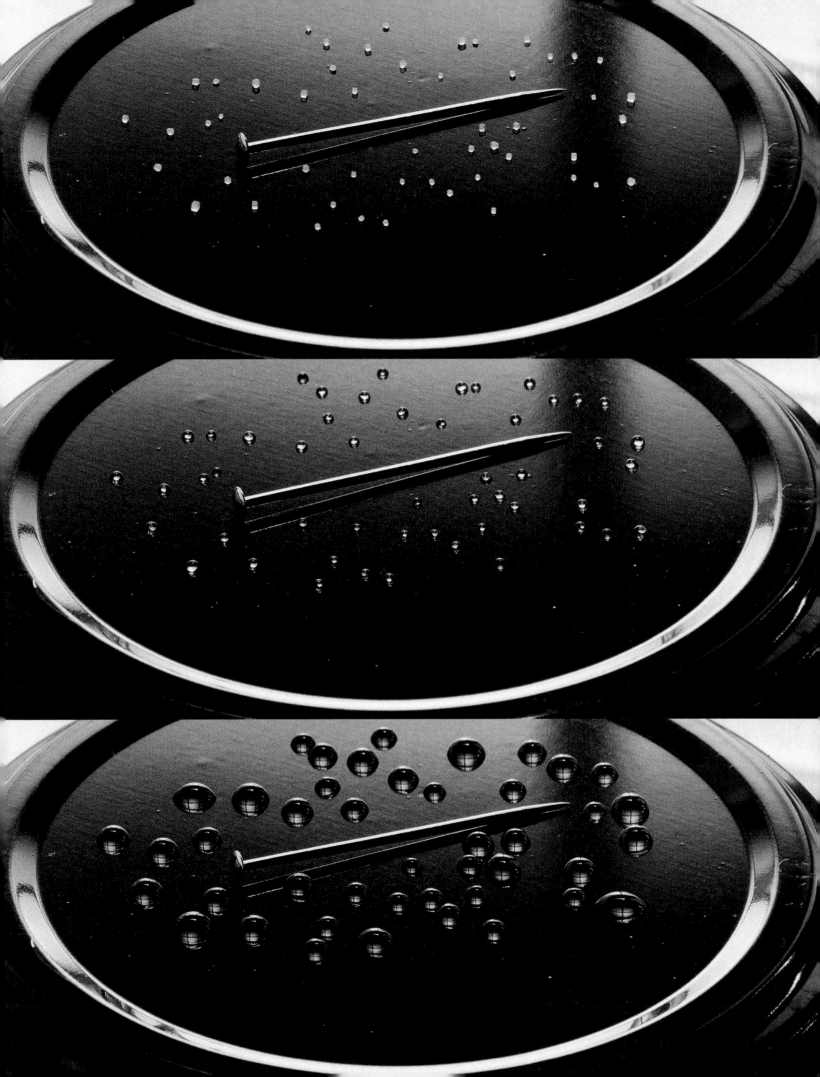

SNOWFLAKES

This snowflake is shown 60 times its actual size. The angles between the six major branches are repeated over and over again in many of the smaller details of this amazing structure. How can such an intricate object form in the sky?

Cloud droplets form when water vapor condenses on particles. But in very cold air, water molecules that cling to particles form tiny ice crystals. As more water molecules from the air freeze onto the crystal, they join at angles that allow a six-sided structure to form. If the crystal grows large enough, it will fall to the ground as a snowflake.

Clouds that produce snow often contain both ice crystals *and* liquid droplets. At the center of this snowflake is a cloud droplet that froze, allowing the snowflake to form around it. Scattered throughout are other cloud droplets that have frozen onto the snowflake as it fell through the cloud.

Sometimes snow mixes with pellets of sleet, which are frozen raindrops like the ones shown below. By contrast, snowflakes are ice crystals that form when water vapor changes directly from a gas to a solid.

SLEET
15 TIMES
ACTUAL SIZE

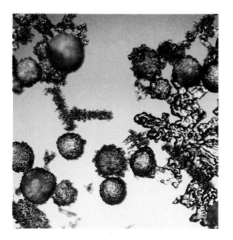

ENDLESS VARIETY

Many ice crystals grow into shapes that are just tiny slivers, rods, or clumps of ice. Of these, the underlying six-sided structure may not always be visible. But when weather conditions are just right, the crystals will grow into an astonishing variety of elaborate six-sided designs.

All the snowflakes on these two pages were photographed on the same day. All share the same angles, but vary in design. One has six branches of unequal length, giving the appearance of a three-sided snowflake. Another snowflake has only four branches. Apparently, two of its branches didn't grow. Odd variations like these are typical. Because different conditions of humidity, wind, and temperature affected the growth of each snowflake as it fell, each design holds secrets of its unique journey to earth.

When a snowflake melts, its intricate design is lost forever in a drop of water. But a snowflake can vanish in another way. It can change directly from ice to vapor. The sequence below shows a single snowflake as it gradually disappears.

SNOWFLAKES
ACTUAL SIZE

FROST AND DEW

On some days, when the air is humid, a sudden drop in temperature during the night will cause water vapor to condense on cold surfaces. By morning, the landscape is covered in sparkling drops of water — dew. If temperatures fall below freezing, the cold-weather relative of dew appears — frost.

On windows, frost forms along tiny scratches and other imperfections in the glass. As with snowflakes, frost is the result of water vapor changing from a gas to a solid. That's why the angular structure of ice crystals is evident in the fern-like patterns of frost.

When dew forms, a short walk through the grass will soak your feet. On spider webs, dewdrops appear like glistening pearls. In this photograph, we can see how water reflects and bends light; an upside-down landscape appears in each drop of water.

WATER AND LIGHT

If you look carefully at this beam of light, you'll see the mysterious way in which light interacts with water.

Some of the light is reflected, which means that it bounces off the surface of the water. But some of the light passes into the water. As the light enters the water, molecules bend the light, or *refract* it. The bent rays of white light are transformed into all the colors of the rainbow.

How is this possible? White light is made up of waves of many different sizes, or *wavelengths*. The shortest wavelength, which we see as violet, bends the most. Red, the longest wavelength, bends the least. All the other colors fall in between.

Sun shining on spray from a garden hose creates a rainbow. The spray produces drops of water that bend the light and flash bright colors when seen from the correct angle. Natural rainbows work exactly the same way. The sun must be behind you and low in the sky. The arc of the rainbow is caused by the sun shining on billions of spherical raindrops that fill the sky.

THE WATER CYCLE

The sun's heat and the earth's gravity keep water in constant motion. Water evaporates from puddles, ponds, lakes, and oceans; from plants and trees; and even from your skin. Water vapor moves invisibly through the air, but it is always ready to condense on a cool blade of grass or the surface of a pond. Massive clouds form as vapor condenses on tiny particles of dust in the air. Then, and only then, can water fall from the sky as rain, replenishing lakes, rivers, and oceans. Hard to predict, impossible to control, water cycles around the earth.

And water is precious. Without it, not a single living thing could survive. No plants would grow, not even one blade of grass. No animals would roam the earth, not even a spider. But somewhere in the world right now, snow drifts on a mountaintop and rain falls in a valley. And all around us, we are reminded of the never ending journey of a drop of water.

An experiment is a question which we ask of Nature, who is always ready to give a correct answer, provided we ask properly, that is, provided we arrange a proper experiment.

—CHARLES VERNON BOYS, 1896

OBSERVATIONS AND EXPERIMENTS

Water's curious behavior has mystified people for centuries. Many of these mysteries have been solved through careful observation and diligent experimentation. Here are some suggestions for how you can make your own observations and experiments.

IMPORTANT PRECAUTIONS

Before doing any experiments, make sure you take the following precautions: Always get permission from an adult to use glassware and any other materials required for the experiment. When working indoors, choose an area, such as a kitchen countertop, that won't be harmed by accidental spills. Remove any items that would be damaged from water or handling with wet hands. Never use water near electrical outlets or appliances. When doing experiments involving sunlight, never stare directly into the sun; this could cause very serious damage to your eyes. Always work safely; clean up spills and put away materials in their proper places when you are done.

MOLECULES IN MOTION

This is easy to do and beautiful to watch. For the best visibility, use a clear glass or jar of any size. Fill it with clean water. When the water is absolutely still, carefully add a drop of food coloring. The molecules of coloring separate as they move among the molecules of water.

ICE

Ice expands when it freezes because water molecules need more space to align themselves in the rigid structure of ice. If you wish to freeze water in a container as an experiment, do not use glass. The expansion of the ice will crack the glass.

SURFACE TENSION

To 'float' a steel pin, use a shallow bowl of water. (It's easier to retrieve the pin if it sinks.) Bend a paper clip to make a holder for the pin. Gently lower the pin into the water with the paper clip. With practice, you can float a paper clip, too.

CAPILLARY ATTRACTION

The experiment on page 13 works best with very narrow glass tubes. But there are other ways you can watch capillary attraction at work. Place a drop of water on a dry plate. Then, very carefully, touch the top of the drop with a paper towel. The drop will spread rapidly through the tiny spaces between the paper's fibers.

SOAP BUBBLES

To make a bubble formula, add a third cup of liquid dish washing soap to a quart of cold water. Stir gently and you're ready to go. For longer lasting bubbles, add 2 tablespoons of glycerin (available at drugstores).

Beautiful colors can be observed in soap films. An easy way to do this is to dip the rim of a glass or jar into your bubble formula. When you pull it out, a soap film will be stretched across the opening. Angle the film toward a window or a bright light and watch for the changing colors. The colors are caused by the way light interacts with the very thin film. This phenomenon is called *interference*.

To get a bubble to rest on a stand, wet the rim of a small glass or jar with the bubble formula. Then, blow a bubble and catch it on the rim and set the glass down gently. If you wet a pin with the bubble formula, you can drop it into the glass without breaking the bubble!

A large, clear container can be used as a protective cover to make your bubble last much longer. Cover your bubble as it rests on the stand and it will last for several hours. Just before it breaks, the bubble will become so thin, it will look like a faint apparition.

BUBBLE FRAMES

The wire stand and frames on pages 16 and 17 were made from brass wire, soldered at the joints. Pipe cleaners, which can be twisted together, are an excellent substitute. You can make a blower with a pipe cleaner, plastic pipe, or cardboard tube.

Bend pipe cleaners into any shape frame you wish. Try to predict what the film will look like before you dip it in the bubble formula. Then, test your theory.

CONDENSATION

In humid weather, you can watch water condense on the cold outer surface of a glass of ice water. In cold weather, there is usually much less water vapor in the air, and you may not see water condensing on the glass. But if you put an *empty* glass in the freezer for about thirty minutes, then take it out, you will see it frost over from condensation.

CONDENSATION AND EVAPORATION

You can do the experiment on page 25 in just about any weather. Spray clean water on a cookie sheet. Place a glass upside down so it covers some, but not all, of the drops. Think about what happens both outside and inside the glass.

You can modify this experiment to see how cloud droplets condense on a particle. Sprinkle a few salt grains on a bottle cap. Place the bottle cap among the droplets and cover it with a glass. After several minutes, you will see water condensing on the salt grains. After an hour or so, water droplets will dissolve the salt. Remove the glass cover and let the droplets evaporate. Will the salt disappear or will it remain?

CONDENSATION NUCLEI

Airborne particles that cloud droplets form on are called *condensation nuclei*. Salt works in this experiment because water vapor sticks to it, even at room temperature. Other types of condensation nuclei, such as soil particles, must be in cold air for the vapor to stick. You can replace the salt with sand, but the droplets are not likely to form unless they are very cold.

To get an idea of how tiny condensation nuclei really are, look at the cloud droplets embedded in the snowflake on page 29. The particles, whether salt or soil, can be hundreds of times smaller than the droplets themselves.

SNOWFLAKES

If you happen to live where it snows, you can use a magnifying glass to study different types of snow. Dress appropriately for cold weather because you will have to stay outdoors or in an unheated shelter. Use a pocket mirror to catch snowflakes as they fall. Press the snowflake gently to the mirror with a feather or a wooden toothpick. Angle the mirror to catch the best light and look at the snowflakes with a magnifying glass.

DEW

If your local evening weather report forecasts dew, you will have a chance to observe how dew condenses early the next morning. Wear waterproof shoes or boots when you go exploring. In open yards or fields, it's easy to find tiny spider webs in the grass. With the sun at your back, watch for flashes of color in the dewdrops. If you position yourself just right, you will see all the colors of the rainbow refracting in the dewdrops of a spider's web.

REFRACTION

You can refract light into rainbow colors as on page 34 on a sunny day at any time of the year. Fill a cylindrical, clear-sided glass of any size with water. Place the glass in a sunny window and watch for the rainbow on the floor. If you darken the room and make a slit in a piece of cardboard that covers the window, the colors will appear very bright.

If the sunlight does not come through at the proper angle, use a pocket mirror to redirect the sunlight.

RAINBOWS

In early morning or late afternoon on a sunny day, you can make a rainbow with a garden hose. Adjust the nozzle so the water comes out in a fine spray. With the sun at your back, spray the water in the air in front of you. When you see the rainbow, notice that it moves when you do and that the shadow of your head is always at the center of the arc. This is also true of naturally occurring rainbows.

SPHERICAL RAINDROPS

If you don't mind getting a little wet, you can see how spray from the hose produces the spherical drops of water that make rainbows possible. With the nozzle adjusted for a fine spray, turn the valve on the spigot to lower the pressure. Point the nozzle straight up to make a miniature fountain. You will clearly see the spherical drops of water dancing at the top of the fountain.

THINK OF YOUR OWN EXPERIMENTS

If you have questions about what you've learned, think about how you can devise an experiment to answer them. For example, on page 15, it is stated that surface tension is weakened by soap. Is that true? You can test the accuracy of that statement with an experiment: After successfully floating a paper clip on water, repeat the same experiment with bubble formula to find the answer.

ABOUT THIS BOOK

For more than 20 years, I have worked as a photographer. Very often, I use special effects to create photographs that are intended to look as if improbable or impossible things happen. To do this, I modify cameras and lights, build sets, and construct models. I also experiment with a variety of materials, and make careful observations to learn how things work. Consequently, the technical challenges of this art form have led me toward a greater awareness of science.

Out of curiosity, I began to collect old science books. Most of them were written for children about 100 years ago. I became fascinated with the way these books used illustrations to depict simple, but clever, science experiments. And there was something else I noticed about these illustrations. Even the simplest experiments appeared as if improbable or impossible things were happening. Intrigued, I recreated some of the experiments and photographed them with my camera. The results seemed magical, but not because of any photographic trick; it was only the forces of nature at work. It was from these explorations that the idea for this book emerged.

The photographs in this book were made by conventional methods and are faithful to the science described in the text. The photographs of snowflakes are of real snowflakes, and no substitute for water has been used. With the exception of a few minor color adjustments, no photographs were altered.

Many of the experiments in this book are the same as, or similar to, those used in books that introduced science to children nearly 100 years ago: in particular, *Soap Bubbles and the Forces That Mold Them*, written in 1896 by the ingenious British scientist Charles Vernon Boys; *A Study of Splashes*, written in 1908 by A.M. Worthington, who was the first person to make stop-motion photographs of water splashes; and *The Fairy-Land of Science*, written in 1878 by Arabella B. Buckley. Also, techniques for photographing the snowflakes in this book were obtained from the published work of W.A. Bentley, of Jericho, Vermont, who made the first extensive photographs of snowflakes, beginning in 1885.

—WALTER WICK